Amazing
Cats

WRITTEN BY
ALEXANDRA PARSONS

PHOTOGRAPHED BY
JERRY YOUNG

Dorling Kindersley · London

A Dorling Kindersley Book

Project editors Helen Parker and Christine Webb
Senior art editor Jacquie Gulliver
Managing editor Sophie Mitchell
Editorial director Sue Unstead
Art director Colin Walton

Special photography by Jerry Young
Illustrations by Gill Elsbury, Julie Anderson, and John Hutchinson
Animals supplied by Trevor Smith's Animal World
Editorial consultants The staff of the Natural History Museum, London
Special thanks to the Cat Survival Trust

First published in Great Britain in 1990 by
Dorling Kindersley Limited
9 Henrietta Street, London WC2E 8PS

Reprinted 1991

British Library Cataloguing in Publication Data
Parsons, Alexandra
Amazing cats
1. Cats
I. Title
636.8

ISBN 0-86318-472-3

Colour reproduction by Colourscan, Singapore
Typeset by Windsorgraphics, Ringwood, Hampshire
Printed in Italy by A. Mondadori Editore, Verona

Contents

What is a cat?

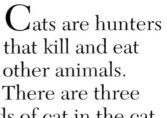

Cats are hunters that kill and eat other animals. There are three kinds of cat in the cat family tree – big cats like the lion; small cats like bobcats and your pet cat; and the cheetah, which has a branch all to itself.

Wild cat

Lion

Tiger

Black panther

Ocelot   Bobcat

Cheetah

Leopard

Watch out!
All cats see well at night. By day the centre of the eye, which lets in light, is narrow and slit-like, but at night it is big and round.

day

night

Clever puss
Cats are known for their cleverness. In the old story of Puss in Boots, a crafty cat helps his young master to marry a beautiful princess. He wins over her father, the king, with gifts of delicious food.

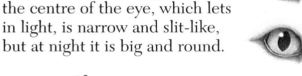

A good stretch
A cat's skeleton has about 40 more bones than yours, and a very flexible spine. This is why cats are so agile.

Claws in, claws out
When they're not hunting and climbing, cats pull their sharp claws into special pockets to protect them.

pulled in

pushed out

Help!
Using their sharp claws and strong legs, all cats (like this leopard cat) can climb *up* trees in a flash. But some pet cats have trouble climbing *down*!

This is no leopard
It has a spotted coat like a leopard's. But this leopard cat is actually a small cat that lives and hunts in the forests of Asia.

Black cat
This black tomcat spends a lot of time fighting with other male cats who stray into the area where he lives. This area is called his territory.

The pharaohs' cat

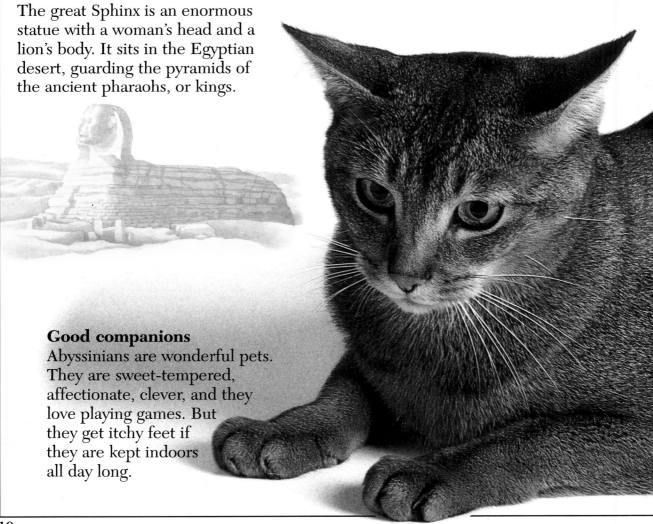

The proud-looking Abyssinian is a pet with an exotic past. It is, probably, related to the sacred cat of ancient Egypt, which was worshipped a long, long time ago.

A working agreement
The Egyptians pampered and protected their sacred cats. In return, the cats kept mice out of the grain stores.

Stone cat
The great Sphinx is an enormous statue with a woman's head and a lion's body. It sits in the Egyptian desert, guarding the pyramids of the ancient pharaohs, or kings.

Good companions
Abyssinians are wonderful pets. They are sweet-tempered, affectionate, clever, and they love playing games. But they get itchy feet if they are kept indoors all day long.

Multicoloured coat

Abyssinians come in many colours. If you look closely at their fur, you will see that each hair has stripes of two or three different colours.

silver   *blue*   *normal*   *lilac*

Making music

The Abyssinian cat would be the star in any cats' choir. Its musical miaow sounds more like a birdcall than a catcall.

Each hair has two or three bands of colour

A good licking

Cats clean their fur with their tongues, teeth, and paws.

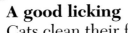

A long fur coat

Longhair cats may have originally come from cold countries like Russia, where their fur coats keep them warm. Their beautiful long fur needs a lot of care and attention.

Hot property
Legend says that the sacred Birman cat was found only in Burma. But one day, an American millionaire smuggled some home with him.

Wild ancestor
Our pet cats' wild relative, the manul, can hoot like an owl and yelp like a dog!

Dipped in paint
This bundle of fur is a seal colourpoint longhair. Colourpoint means that her face, ears, legs, and tail are tipped with another colour, in this case a lovely warm seal-brown.

Pass the hairbrush
A longhair cat needs all the help it can get to keep its mop of fur clean and untangled. Just like our hair, it needs to be combed and brushed every day.

Handle with care
A cat likes to be picked up just so. Put one hand behind the front legs and scoop up the cat's bottom, supporting its body.

Cats turn their ear-flaps to pick up the tiniest sound

Head over heels
One sniff of a plant called catnip is enough to send cats crazy – they roll about and rub the scent of the leaves all over them.

Pardon!
Cats don't just nibble grass because it tastes good. It helps them vomit food they don't want, or fur they've swallowed while grooming.

Jungle ocelot

This cat's beautiful fur is the cause of all its problems. Ocelot fur makes expensive coats, so ocelots have been hunted almost to extinction.

How did you get your spots?
Spots help to disguise, or camouflage, cats. But no one knows why every cat has different spots.

Jaguar

Cheetah

Leopard

Clouded leopard

Rare cat
Ocelots are very rare. If you want to see one in the wild, you will have to go to the rain forests of South America.

14

Sleeping platform

Ocelots are excellent climbers and can scale a tree in no time at all. Sometimes they even sleep up in the branches.

Day and night

Ocelots usually stalk their prey at night. But if the hunting is good, they will come out during the day to make the best of it.

Hard to spot

With its fur blending in with the leafy shadows, the ocelot can sneak up on the rats and lizards that scuttle about on the forest floor.

On the scent

To warn other cats to keep out of its territory, a cat sprays the boundaries with urine. It will also scratch and rub its head and feet against trees and bushes, marking them with scent from special glands.

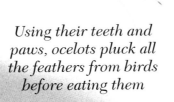

Using their teeth and paws, ocelots pluck all the feathers from birds before eating them

15

Bobcat

This little wild cat lives in forests and deserts. In the summer, its coat is brown. But when the snows come, the coat grows longer and turns greyish-white.

Baby den
Baby bobcats, or kits, are born in a den. The mother usually has two kits in her litter.

Bobtail
The bobcat is a kind of lynx. Lynxes have spotted fur, pointed ears, and little beards, or ruffs. The bobcat gets its name from its short, stubby bobtail.

Cats feel their way with the help of their whiskers

Here, there, and everywhere
North America is the bobcat's home. It lives in many different places: from the hot, dry deserts of Mexico to the cold, snowy mountains of Canada and the marshy swamps of Florida.

The goddess Venus and the cat

Venus once changed a cat into a woman so that she could marry a handsome man. But when she spotted a mouse, the poor woman couldn't resist chasing it. Immediately, she became a cat again.

Forest hunter

Bobcats hunt at night, creeping up and pouncing with a huge bound on rabbits, birds, or even small deer.

Glowing eyes

Have you seen a cat's eyes glowing in the dark? They glow because a special layer inside the eye, the tapetum, bounces light back like a mirror.

large back feet for snow-walking

Hide-and-seek

The bobcat often lives near towns. It is so swift and quiet that most people don't know when there's a bobcat about.

King of beasts

Lions are huge and powerful wild cats. They don't miaow like pet cats. Lions have special voice boxes so they can roar very loudly and deeply to scare enemies.

Family life
Lions live on the hot, grassy plains of Africa in groups called prides. They are the only cats that live together like a family.

Lady killers
Female lions, or lionesses, are smaller than males. They bring up the cubs and do most of the hunting. Quietly they stalk an animal and circle it. All of a sudden they charge, knock it to the ground, and kill it with a bite to the throat.

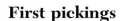

Hunting tools
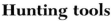
Lions can see, smell, and hear better than humans. They also have powerful jaws with strong, sharp teeth for slicing through meat.

The whip hand
People have been keeping lions for hundreds of years, but they are still not easy to tame.

First pickings
Although the lionesses catch the food, the male lion has first pickings. When he has eaten his fill, the rest of the family joins in.

A good turn
A boy called Androcles once helped a wild lion by pulling a thorn out of its paw. Soon after, he was captured by the Romans and thrown to the lions. But he was saved by one of the lions – the same one he had helped before.

Defending the family
Male lions have big, thick manes of hair which make them look even bigger and fiercer. Their main job is to defend the pride and its territory.

The lion's sharp claws can be pulled right in

19

Spot the leopard

When they're not out hunting, these strong and graceful cats spend a lot of time lazing about in trees. Sadly, many leopards are killed each year for their beautiful spotted fur.

Nursery school
Leopard cubs stay with their mother until they are between one and two years old. They learn how to hunt and kill.

Spotted friend
In ancient legends and paintings, leopards were often used as a sign of strength and beauty. Bacchus, the Greek god of wine, was often shown with one of these beautiful and powerful creatures at his side.

Its spotted fur helps the leopard hide in the jungles of Africa

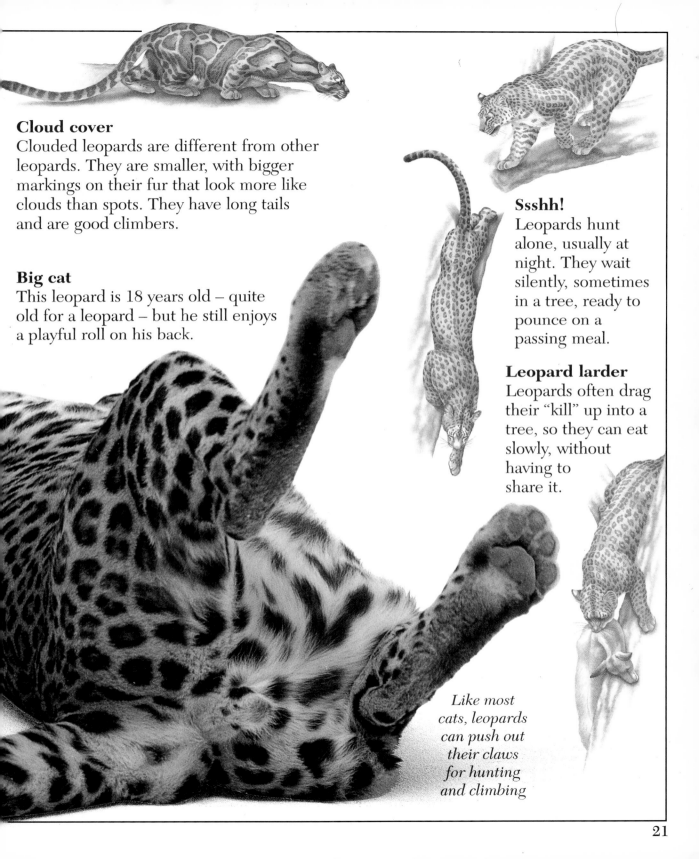

Cloud cover
Clouded leopards are different from other leopards. They are smaller, with bigger markings on their fur that look more like clouds than spots. They have long tails and are good climbers.

Big cat
This leopard is 18 years old – quite old for a leopard – but he still enjoys a playful roll on his back.

Ssshh!
Leopards hunt alone, usually at night. They wait silently, sometimes in a tree, ready to pounce on a passing meal.

Leopard larder
Leopards often drag their "kill" up into a tree, so they can eat slowly, without having to share it.

Like most cats, leopards can push out their claws for hunting and climbing

A cat that swims?

Most pet cats hate water and will scratch and hiss rather than get wet. But the Turkish swimming cat loves to swim, especially in warm, shallow streams or pools.

The fur is smooth, silky, and slightly oily to make it more waterproof

No vest
The Turkish swimming cat has no woolly undercoat like other longhaired cats. This means that its wet fur dries out much more quickly.

Holy cat
Turkish swimming cats all have a white patch on their foreheads. Turkish people used to believe that this mark was the thumbprint of their god, Allah.

Cold comfort

These cats come from Lake Van in the Turkish mountains. In winter their coats grow longer to keep them warm in the bitterly cold weather.

Gone fishing

Many wild cats think nothing of getting wet if it means they can catch a tasty fish or frog. This fishing cat from China even has special webbed paws for swimming.

Summer wardrobe

Turkish swimming cats lose their long fur coats in the hot Turkish summer. This is called moulting. It can be a very messy business as the hairs get everywhere.

Most Turkish swimming cats have pale amber eyes

A wet, pink nose is the sign of a healthy cat

Travelling cats

Sailors used to think that a black cat on board ship brought them good luck. It certainly kept away the rats!

Desert caracal

This fierce-looking cat comes from the deserts of Africa and Asia. It has short fur to help it keep cool, and can go for a long time without a drink.

Help with the hunt
A long time ago, in India, people trained caracals to catch gazelles and birds for them.

Desert stalker
The caracal does most of its hunting at night. It has to be very fast to catch its prey of hares, birds, lizards, and small antelope.

Dinner flies past
Caracals are so good at jumping that they can catch a bird as it takes off. In India, contests are held with tame caracals to see which can strike down the most pigeons in one leap.

Standing snack
Sometimes a caracal will stand up on its hind legs to eat – not like a cat at all.

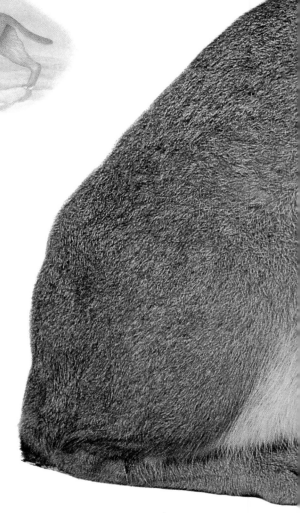

The word caracal means "black ears" in Turkish

The sand cat
This desert cat has mats of hair under its paws to protect it from the burning rocks and sand.

Born blind
Like most kittens, baby caracals are born with their eyes closed.

Paws for thought
Cats have five toes on their front feet. But the fifth toe doesn't touch the ground, so it leaves no mark.

front paw print

fifth toe

claws in   *claws out*

25

Forest wild cat

Wild cats may look like pet tabby cats – but they're not. They're ferocious, much more powerful, and hard to tame. They live in thick forests and on craggy mountains – far away from people.

All alone
The wild cat guards its own special hunting area. It has its own tracks and paths, cosy places to sleep, and favourite claw-sharpening trees. It won't let any other wild cat hunt there.

Fierce kittens
Female wild cats give birth to four or five kittens. At first the kittens look cute and playful, but at three months they're snarling just like their parents.

Charming!
When a wild cat is angry, it flattens its ears right down and curls back its lips to show its long, sharp front teeth.

Wildcat strike
A sudden strike in a factory is sometimes called a wildcat strike.

Keep your fur on!
When a cat is scared, it arches its back, lowers its tail, and makes all the hairs on its body stand on end.

The wild cat's markings make it hard to see in the forest

Gone fishing
Like most pet cats, wild cats love fish. They will sometimes spend hours on end going in and out of the water to catch them.

Shadowy figures
One kind of wild cat lives in the forests and highlands of Scotland. During the day it hides and sleeps in dens among the rocks and trees and when it sneaks out at night, it keeps to the shadows.

Nine lives

Cats are agile and fast, and always seem to land on their feet when they're in a tight spot. They can jump a gap twice the length of their body with no trouble at all. They are such good survivors that people often say they have nine lives.

On the prowl
Like all cats, this ginger tom walks on "tiptoe". Its body is stretched out and close to the ground, ready to leap or pounce at a moment's notice.

Cats are such good balancers, that they can walk along a strip of wood as narrow as a tightrope

The great leap
Cats move just like ballet dancers. They even jump gracefully. With a huge push from the back legs, this cat launches into the air. Using its tail for balance, it stretches out for the ground, and touches down with its front legs first.

Top sprinter

The cheetah's slender body is specially built for speed, making it the fastest animal on land. At full speed it is thought to sprint at 90 km/h.

Practice makes perfect

Catching dinner isn't as easy as it looks. Cats have to be strong, alert, and very swift. Even pet cats spend a lot of time learning to stalk and kill mice and birds.

Cat burglars

Some thieves are nimble, good at scaling walls, squeezing into tiny gaps, and then making a quick getaway. That's why they are called cat burglars, after some of the best climbers around.

Index